AN ILLUSTRATED GUIDE
TRACTOR

CW00337051

IAN WESTWELL

CONTENTS

INTRODUCTION   6

AGCO   24

Dt Series   26
Lt Series   28
Rt Series   30

ARMATRAK   32

604 Series   34

BUHLER   36

200 Series   38
Genesis Series   40
Htt Series   42

CASE   44

Magnum Series   46
Maxxum Series   48
Puma Series   50
Steiger Series   52

CLAAS   54

Ares Series   56
Axion Series   58
Xerion Trac   60

DEUTZ-FAHR   62

Agrolux 57-67   64
Agrotron Ttv   66

FENDT   68

700 Series   70
800 Series   72

HÜRLIMANN   74

X Series   76

JOHN DEERE   78

6000 Series   80
7000 Series   82
8000 Series   84
9000 Series   86

LAMBORGHINI   88

R Series   90
Speciality Series   92

MASSEY FERGUSON   94

500 Series   96
5400 Series   98
6400 Series   100
7400 Series   102
8600 Series   104

SAME   106

20-99 Hp   108
100-299 Hp   110

INTRODUCTION

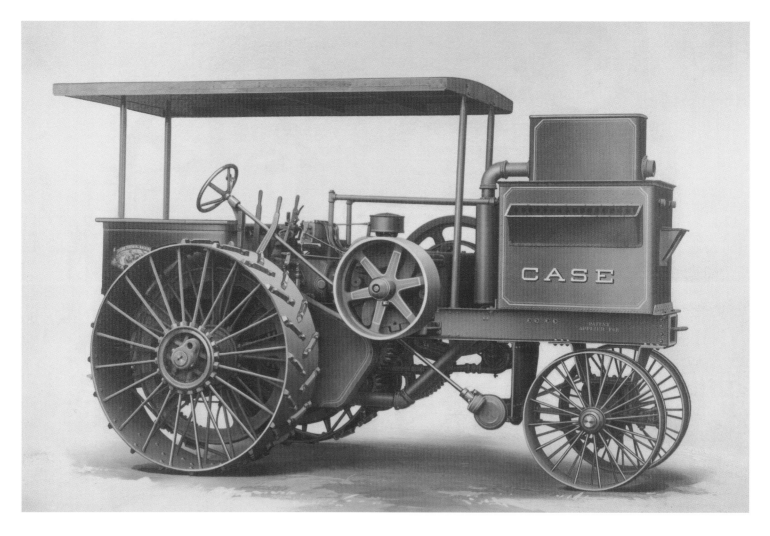

THE DAWN OF THE TRACTOR

The mechanization of farming is by now largely an excepted fact yet the tractor that is now the cornerstone of this mechanization is little more than a century old. Their history really begins with the development of a viable steam engine in the first decades of nineteenth century. These early machines were initially used to tow various implements, such as threshing machines, to their place of use and then power them when they were being used. However, the age of the steam traction engine was relatively short-lived and the writing on the wall was actually there from 1859—the year that oil was found in the United States and both

kerosene and petrol was distilled from it. Matters progressed in 1890 when the patents of Nikolaus Otto's four-stroke petrol-driven internal combustion engine expired, thereby allowing anyone to develop this new form of power.

Tractor manufacturers were soon developing petrol-driven types. The Waterloo Gasoline Traction Engine founded in Iowa by John Froelich was a case in point. He built a machine powered by a single-cylinder Van Duzen engine and in 1916 introduced the Waterloo Boy, which is widely regarded as the first truly successful petrol-powered machine. These new machines finally acquired a new name in 1906 when Hart-Parr, an Iowa-based enterprise that had produced its first petrol-driven design some four years earlier, coined the term "tractor."

The story of tractor manufacture involved literally scores if not hundreds of small-scale manufacturers, chiefly in North America and Europe. Europe's early pioneers involved some long gone companies but also some that have survived in one form or another down the ages. These included the likes of Albone and Saunderson in England, Fendt and Deutz in Germany, De Souza in France and Landini in Italy. The number of producers rocketed immediately after the end of World War I. For example, there were just six tractor manufacturers in the United States in 1905 but that figure had risen to nearly 190 by 1921. Yet many of the smaller manufacturers were soon suffering, not least because of the Great Depression.

Tractors had previously been large and costly but it soon became clear that what farmer's really needed were smaller and cheaper models. The truth was that handcrafted machines produced in limited numbers by small manufacturers could never reach the levels of production that would bring unit costs down. Standardized mass production was the way forward and, although some firms soldiered on, the tractor market became increasingly dominated by a smaller number of larger concerns. Some, like the Ford Motor Company, already existed but others emerged through a process of mergers and acquisitions. The U.S. market gradually became dominated by a handful of such companies and by 1933 there were just nine major manufacturers in the United States. These worked hard to keep in front of each other by making frequent innovations.

Ford Motor Company saw the potential of the tractor early and in 1907 introduced the prototype of what it hoped would be the first mass-produced design. It took some ten years for the tractor, the Fordson (Henry Ford and Son) Model F, to go into production. The design proved a huge hit and, although it was not as inexpensive as Ford had wanted, it nevertheless sold well—some 35,000 by 1919—and it captured something like 70 percent of the U.S. tractor market. Ford eventually transferred

production to Europe, first settling in Ireland during 1919 and then moving to England in 1933. The next great Fordson was 1939's Model 9N. Something like 99,000 of these were produced in just three years but even these sales were dwarfed by the Model 2N, some 200,000 of which were sold between 1942 and 1947.

The J. I. Case Threshing Company of Wisconsin, which had been founded in 1863 as J. I. Case and Company in order to construct steam engines, produced its first experimental petrol-driven design in 1892. It was not a great success, more of a marker for the future and Case actually developed its first

viable machine, the large Case 30-60, in 1911. This won the Winnipeg Tractor Trials and remained in production until 1916. A smaller version, the 12-25 was manufactured in 1913 but the Case 20-40 was the better machine. Case flirted with a three-wheeled design, the 10-20 Crossmotor, and some 5000 were sold between 1915 and 1922 but it was the light-weight, four-wheeled 9-18 that really made the company. It was introduced in 1916 and something like 6000 of its two variants, the 9-18A and 9-18B, had sold within three years.

Further successes followed. The 10-18 made its debut in 1917 and some 900 were sold in three years, while 1919's 15-27 did even better, with Case selling some 17,500 units by 1924. That year also saw the arrival of a new company president, Leon Clausen, and he ordered a new range of tractor. The Case Model L arrived in 1929 and remained in production for some ten years, when it was replaced by the Model LA, a remarkable design that was produced until the mid-1950s. Case also introduced the Model C at the same time as the Model L and it helped to open the British market to Case. It performed well at the World Tractor Trials held in Oxfordshire during 1930s and proved so successful that it was offered in a variety of guises—the Models CC (row crop), CI (industrial), CO (orchard), CV (Vineyard) and CD

(crawler). In the years before World War II Case also introduced the four-wheeled Model D and the tricycle DC and followed these with the Models S and V.

International Harvester was created through the merger of Deering and Mc , two small-scale tractor makers, in 1902 and the new concern began selling two designs, the Titan and Mogul through Deering and McCormick dealerships respectively. The first true International Harvester design, the Type A, appeared in 1906 and this soldiered on until the Type B was introduced some 10 years later. The company also made inroads into Europe, especially Britain, where 1914's paraffin-powered Titan 10-20 was popular. The International Harvester 8-16, which was equally popular and was produced between 1917 and 1922. Other models, like the 15-30 and 10-20 followed shortly after World War I had ended, despite the on set of recession. Both had been designed to take on Fordson inexpensive models and the 10-20, which arrived in 1923, proved a remarkable success selling in excess of 215,000 units by 1942. It was also the basis for International Harvester's first foray into the crawler market, the TracTracTor of 1928 which became the T-20 in 1931.

By this stage the company was a major concern. It had begun producing the Farmell series, the first true crop row tractor, in 1924. This was superseded by the three-tractor Farmell Regular range, which comprised the F-12, F-20 and F-30. The company

also replaced the aging 15-30 with the 22-36 in 1929, although the 10-20 soldiered on until the eve of World War II. International Harvester produced its first diesel-powered tractor, the WD-40, in 1934, the same year that the 22-36 was replaced by the W-30. A new range of tractors was announced in 1940, beginning with the W6, a design which was followed by the W4 and W9.

Allis-Chalmers of Milwaukee had been around since in the late 1840s in one form or another and was given a makeover in 1912. A mere two years later the company produced its first petrol tractor, the tricycle Model 10-18. The business did not actually have its own network of dealerships and fewer than 3000 Model 10-18 were sold, although some did reach France where they were marketed as the Globe tractor. The Model 10-18 was replaced by the more conventional Model 18-30 in 1919. Allis-Chalmers did not easily achieve mass production but matters improved as it began to acquire companies during the period of recession that followed World War I.

Among these was the Monarch Tractor Company of Illinois, which had begun producing crawler tractor in 1917. These included the small Lightfoot 6-10 and the substantially bigger Monarch 75. A staggering 32 farming-related companies, Allis-Chalmers among them, amalgamated in 1929 to form the United Tractor and Equipment Company. Allis-Chalmers was required to produce a new tractor and came up with the United. The parent company did not laste for long but Allis-Chalmers survived and

INTRODUCTION

continued to market the Universal but as the Model U. Both it and the Model E became the cornerstone of the company's business in the early 1930s. The Model E was replaced by the Model A from 1936 while the Model B introduced a year later went on to be a good seller. The Model U received an upgrade in 1936.

John Deere had a long pedigree in the manufacture of farming equipment and in 1918 bought the Waterloo Gasoline Engine company of Iowa, an acquisition that also made it a builder of tractors. Deere continued producing Waterloo's Model N until 1924 but released the Model D in the 1920s. This two-cylinder design proved immensely popular and the basic design was subsequently upgrade until the early 1950s by which time some 160,000 had been built Deere did not rest on its laurels and in 1928 brought out a row crop tractor, the Model GP (General Purpose). This was not wholly successful so the company went back to the drawing board and came up with the tricycle Model GPWT (General Purpose Wide Tread). This proved more popular and various other types were manufactured, including the GPO (General Purpose Orchard) and GP-P (General Purpose-Potato).

Deere boomed in the 1930s, the Great Depression not withstanding. The tricycle Model A arrived in 1934 and continued to pour out of the factory until as late as 1952 by which time a staggering 328,000 had been built. The smaller Model B followed in 1935 and also stayed in production until 1952. Despite these two models, Deere's tractor had not evolved greatly since the 1920s but in 1937 the company began a succession of updated ranges. The new Models A and B arrived in 1937 and were followed by the Model D and H in 1939 and the powerful Model G in 1942.

Minneapolis-Moline grew out of a merger between three companies. The Minneapolis Steel and Machinery, Minneapolis Threshing Machine Company and Moline Implement Company combined in 1929 to form the Minneapolis-Moline Power Implement Company. All of the three companies had been involved in tractor manufacture at one time or another. The company that would become Moline Implement Company bought Ohio's Universal Tractor Company in 1915 and subsequently produced tractors such as the Moline Universal Tractor. The Minneapolis threshing Machine Company had actually built steam traction engines from 1889 and was building tractors by 1911. These included the17-30 Types A and B. Minneapolis Steel and Machinery also produced tractors, introducing the Twin City 40 as early as 1908.

Twin City Tractors was chosen to spearhead Minneapolis-Moline's breakthrough into the market. Minneapolis-Moline went on to introduce a wide number of designs before World War II. These the Universal Model J, a row crop tractor that first appeared in 1935, and the Model U that was first tested at the Nebraska tractor trial in 1938. The latter model came in tricycle form and with standard tread and one version, the UDLX, was available with a cab.

Oliver was the outcome of a merger between four enterprises in 1929, when Hart-Parr, Nichols and Shepherd, the American Seeding Machine Company and the Oliver Chilled Plow Company combined to form the Oliver Farm Equipment Sales Company. The new business introduced two row crop tractors, the Oliver Hart Parr Models A and B, which came in several versions (Standard, Western, Ricefield and Orchard) and remained in production until 1937. The company also produced the Oliver Hart-Parr Row Crop 70 HC in 1935 and the updated Oliver 90 (the Hart-Parr name was dropped in 1937). In 1940 it began selling a smaller tractor, the Oliver 60.

Caterpillar grew out of various experiment conducted in the late 19th century by Benjamin Holt and Daniel Best, who both tried to wed tracks to steam traction engines to produce what was then termed "crawlers". The first such experiment with a completed steam crawler took place in 1904 and just two years later the original petrol-powered crawler made its debut. Holt's Caterpillar tractors undertook sterling work during World War I and in 1921 he introduced the peacetime Best 30 Tracklayer. Holt and Best merged in 1925 and the caterpillar Tractor company was born. Various other types of caterpillar tractor soon arrived including the Caterpillar Twenty in 1927 and the Caterpillar Fifteen in 1929. The 1930s saw the debut of the Diesel Sixty-Five and a new range of diesel-powered types, the RD series, including the RD4 RD6, RD7 and RD 8. These were all rather large machine but in 1938 Caterpillar issued the small D2, which was aimed squarely at farmers.

THE ERA OF THE GREAT MANUFACTURERS

At the outbreak of World War II on September 1, 1939, Britain had just three main makers of tractors and their expertise was immediately utilized in the manufacture of war goods. However Britain needed to increase its agricultural output, not least because of the menace posed by German U-boats, and turned to the United States for ever more tractors under the Lend-Lease scheme. This was a boon time for the larger U.S. manufacturers and saw them emerge as the dominant force in tractor manufacture, a position that they would reinforce once the conflict had ended.

Yet some would themselves disappear over the next few decades as "merger mania" took hold. Minneapolis-Moline, for example, was a leading player before the war and, indeed went on to produce some successful post-war designs, including Models G and GB, which were updates of 1939's Model GT. It soldiered on into the 1960s, introducing models like the M-5 in 1960. Yet in 1963, less than two decades after the end of the war, it was swallowed up by the White Motor Company. It was

a fate that would befall several other previous top dogs of U.S. tractor manufacture in the post-war world.

Allis-Chalmers introduced their Model B tractor with pneumatic tyres in 1938 and it was a huge hit, so much so that after the war it was built in Britain for both the home and export markets. The tricycle Model C, which was built between 1940 and 1948, was also a good seller. The company, like many others, introduced a plethora of new designs in the postwar world. There were the Models G and WD and the WD-45 which was fitted with a petrol engine. Then came a variant of the WD-45 in 1955, which was something of a landmark for Allis-Chalmers as it was their first diesel-engined tractor. Farmers were sufficiently impressed to buy something like 85,000 of them. The company's involvement with British farming also strengthened after 1945. The Model B was considered something of an outdated machine back in the United States but in austerity era Britain it was a godsend, an Allis-Chalmers began to build it from 1948 and an upgraded version, the D270, first at a factory in Southampton and later in Lincolnshire. Further designs followed, including the D272 in 1959 and the ED40 a year later. Sales figures for these models were less than expected and Allis-Chalmers closed its British operation down in 1968.

Despite this setback the company had been booming back in the United States. It had acquired the Gleaner Harvester

Corporation and went on to developed the huge D Series of tractors that ultimately ran to around 50 variants. The D17 was one of the most popular designs and some 63,000 were built in a production life that stretched to 10 years. Others fared less well and the D10 and D12 versions sold less than 10,000 units over the same period. The company went into something of a decline thereafter and was bought by Germany's Klockner-Hunboldt-Deutz in 1985 and thereafter traded as Deutz-Allis.

Ford had been one of the United States major war producers but it tractor division was soon back in action after 1945. It had produced something like 140,000 of its 1941-vintage Model 2N in England alone during the conflict so it was a tried and tested design. It was therefore the basis for the Ford 8N, which was produced between 1947 and 1952. The first truly new tractor was the Fordson E27N, which first appeared as early as 1945 and continued in production until 1951. The 1950s saw other designs arrive, not least the 1953 Model NAA Jubilee built to honor the company's fiftieth birthday, and the 600 and 800 Series of 1958.

The following decades were largely a boom time for Ford's tractor arm. Its factories were turning out designs in various countries around the world and it even opted to acquire a rival, buying New Holland to form Ford New Holland. Tractors

continued to appear with both company's liveries and badges but the company itself was snapped up in 1991 by FiatGeotech to become N.H. Geotech. This was renamed as New Holland Incorporated in 1993 but the company was, by agreement, still permitted to sell Ford-badged tractors until 2001.

Case was firmly committed to the U.S. war effort but was badly hit in 1945 by a prolonged industrial dispute that put back its plans to convert back to tractor production. A series of takeover of firms producing other types of farming machinery backfired somewhat but the takeover of John T. Brown allowed the company to recover. Three new tractors designs—the 500, 400 and 300—emerged in 1953, 1955 and 1960 respectively and were effectively the first really new Case series since the increasingly distant 1930s. The revitalized company now embarked on a round of mergers and acquisitions. It linked up with the American Tractor Corporation in 1957, bought France's Societe Francoise Vierzon in 1960 and then looked to England to buy David Brown Limited in 1972. Even the ownership of Case itself had changed during this period of rapid expansion, with Tenneco Incorporated becoming the new owner in 1969.

Case continued to build tractor and in 1975 introduced the 1410 and 1412 series. Various other models appeared at regular intervals – the "Spirit of '76" Model 1570 in 1976, the Models 70 and 90 Series two years later and the 94 Series in 1983. Case was clearly becoming a big player and it got a whole lot bigger in 1985 when it took over a major rival, International Harvester, to become Case IH. Case IH's first tractors duly arrived the very next year and included such models as 685L and the 1594. Case continued to go from strength to strength and the success story continued with designs like the 1255XL, 1056XL and the 4320. It currently produces a wide range of tractors including the Magnum and Maxxum ranges.

Oliver's post-war history was much less spectacular and it ultimately went the way of International Harvester. Things appeared much rosier during World War II, when the company brought out Ohio's Cletrac, formerly the Cleveland Tractor Company, in 1944, four years later, Oliver's hundredth birthday, it released the Fleetline series—Models 66, 77 and 88. Over the following years Oliver brought out the so-called Super Series that comprised Models 44, 55, 66, 77, 88 and 99. However, Oliver was being eyed by a bigger concern and in 1960 was acquired by the White Motor Corporation. The popular Model 55 remained in production for the rest of the decade.

White continued its expansion over the following year, buying the Cockshutt Farm Equipment Company just two years after taking over Oliver, and followed this with a buy out of Minneapolis-Moline in 1962. Nevertheless, all three firms continued to bring out their own-badged tractors until the late 1960s but a major restructuring led to the creation of White Farm Equipment. White produced various designs in the 1970s but was itself taken over in 1981 but continued to produce tractors under the WFE name. In 1987, White's next owner, Allied Products corporation combine it with the New Idea Farm Equipment Company to form White-New Idea. White is currently part of the AGCO Corporation but its name still appears on the company's tractors.

International Harvester had established a good Name with its W Series of tractors that first appeared in 1940 and returned to their manufacture after World War II. It began by improving the W6, which became available in the early 1950s as either the International Harvester Super W6 or as a Farmall Super W6. New models also soon appeared and the Model A was superseded by the Super A. The company also set up camp in Britain and scored some success with its Farmall M. By the early 1960s International Harvester was prospering and brought out models such as the 404 and 504. The decade and the next were times of fast-moving innovation but the company was paralyzed by the economic recession of the early 1980s and suffered crippling losses. Tenneco Incorporated stepped in during 1984, bought the company and merged it with Case to form Case-IH.

Canada's Massey-Harris, a company founded way back in 1891, made a name for itself before World War II with successful designs like the Challenger, 1930's General Purpose, 1939's Model 101 and the Model 25, which sold well during the 1930s and 1940s. It soon confirmed its status. First came the Model 44, essentially an update of the Challenger and then introduced a new range from 1947, including Models 44, 11, 20, 30 and 55.

The most successful design was the Pony, which also emerged in 1947. More than 120,000 were produced in factories in both Canada and France. The Model 44 was also an international success story and they were manufactured or assembled in both the United States and Britain.

Massey-Harris continued to produce excellent designs in the early 1950s and the company grew even stronger in 1953, when it purchased British-owned Ferguson in 1953. The new company was originally known as Massey-Harris-Ferguson and the two concerns continued to build tractors with their own badges. Thus, for example, the Massey-Harris MH50 and Ferguson 40 looked somewhat different but were essentially the same mechanically as they were based on the Ferguson 35. A greater degree of unity began to emerge in 1957 when the company became simply Massey-Ferguson and produced the Model MF35.

This sparked a round of new designs over the following years that included the MF50, MF65 and MF85. The company continued to prosper throughout the 1970s and 1980s, when new ranges of tractors arrived including the Models 1505 and 1805 in the former decade and 3000 and 5000 Series in the middle of the latter decade. With such a pedigree, Massey-Ferguson was ripe for takeover and in 1994 it was captured by the AGCO

INTRODUCTION

New tractor series continued to appear at regular intervals into the 1990s, a decade which saw the introduction of the 6000, 7000 and 8000 Series. Deere remains a dominant force in tractor production and has a worldwide footprint. It has come a long way since the 33-year-old John Deere, a blacksmith from Vermont, made his first "self-polishing" steel plough way back in 1837.

Tractor Developments In Europe

Various European steam traction pioneers played their part in the mechanization of farming in the years before World War I. The very first tractor developed in Britain was the Hornsby-Akroyd Patent Safety Oil Traction engine and in 1896 it became the first tractor to be bought by an English farmer. Other early pioneers were Albone and Saunderson, who produced designs known as the River Ivel and Saunderson Universal Model G. Saunderson soon became the largest manufacturer outside of the United States but was acquired by another firm, Crossley, in the middle years of the 1920s. Saunderson acquisition established a pattern that was to be repeated time and time again over the following decades.

Corporation but tractors are still-produced in its distinctive red livery and it remains one of the biggest manufacturers in the world.

John Deere hit the ground running after the end of World War II and launched several of its older designs with the Model M in 1947. This tractor was used as the basis for two other units, the crawler Model MC and the tricycle MT that appeared two years later. The company's first diesel-engined tractor, the Model R, made it entry the same year and was effectively a replacement for the pre-war Model D. Production of the latter Model continued into 1954 but it was the last to be designated with a letter as Deere had switched to a numerical system some two years earlier. Therefore there followed in the 1950s and 1960s, the 20, 30, 40, 50, 60, 70 and 80 Series.

The regularity and frequency clearly suggested that John Deere was at the top of the game—and the figures backed this up. The company had something like 23 percent of all U.S. sales in 1959 but that had risen by eleven percent in just five years, meaning that John Deere was selling more than one-third of all the tractors purchase each year. The company also diversified into such fields as various financial services and more specialist agricultural machinery over the following decades but never neglected its core business.

There were scores of small-scale manufacturers across Europe in the interwar period but many did not survive for long. In Britain, for example, three companies came to dominated production by the eve of World War II—Fordson, actually part of Henry Ford's business empire, David Brown and Marshall. The writing was clearly on the wall for small manufacturers and matters did not improve after 1945. This was partly due to the slower pace of farming mechanization in comparison to the United States but it was also due to the war itself. European manufacturers had gone over to war-related production and Britain, for example, simply imported much-needed agricultural tractors from the United States, where tractor manufacture was beginning to be consolidated in the hands of fewer and fewer but very large corporations. When peace returned many European producers found they had lost market share and could not easily compete on price. Some did survive but many simply folded or were bought out by their bigger rivals.

One of the most well-known British tractor makers of the era was David Brown. David Brown Gear Cutters began producing tractors for Harry Ferguson in the 1930s, developing a machine known as the Ferguson-Brown Type A. No more than 1350 of them were ever built and it was withdrawn from production in 1939 and Brown went his own way. His first tractor design, the David Brown Vak-1, was revealed the same year. A slightly upgraded version was unveiled shortly after World War II had ended but the wholly new Cropmaster was introduced in 1947. This proved highly popular, especially the diesel version. Next came the smaller Model 2D in 1955, which was squarely aimed at small-scale agriculture. This tractor design was a clear-cut hit with its intended market and something like 2000 of them were sold over the next six years.

David Brown's next design was the 900 tractor, which made its debut in 1956, but production lasted no more than two years and ended when the 950 arrived. This came with both petrol and diesel engines and was upgraded on several occasions over the next four years. The 950 was superseded by the 880, which was effectively a upgraded version of a tractor introduced alongside the 900 tractor. A somewhat smaller design of the latter, the 850, was made available from 1960 and was manufactured until replaced by the 770 in 1965. David Brown was by this stage coming to the end of its life as an independent producer of tractors and in 1972 was taken over by the U.S. giant Case.

One of the key figures in postwar British tractor manufacture was Harry Ferguson, who developed the three-point hitching device and had a short-lived agreement with an English company, David Brown, in the late 1930s to produce a design that featured his hitching system. Ferguson then reached an agreement with Henry Ford that led to the introduction of the Ford Ferguson 9N in 1939 but this deal broke down acrimoniously amid a flurry of litigation. Ferguson set to building his own tractor designs. He reached an agreement with the chief executive of Standard Motor Company back in England to produce his new designs, the TE (Tractor England) and the TO (Tractor Overseas) models.

The first units began to role of the production line in 1946 and both were similar to the 9N but with more powerful engines,

provided first by Continental and from 1947 by Standard. The TE20, nicknamed the "Grey Fergy" because of its livery, was an immense success. Over the next 10 years something like 500,000 were built in England alone and a further 60,000 were constructed in the United States, where the were designated TO20s, between 1948 and 1951. Ferguson followed the designs with the TO30 series in 1951 and the TO35 three years later but Ferguson's association with the company he established was coming to an end. Ferguson actually sold his company to Canada's Massey Harris in 1953 to form Massey-Harris-Ferguson and, for a while, produced Massey-Harris and Ferguson design in tandem. Harry Ferguson sold all his shares in the company in 1957 and ceased to have any involvement in its day-to-day affairs.

Nuffield was one of the more short-lived English tractor manufacturers. It was the brainchild of William Morris, the noted car designer and philanthropist. Morris had toyed with the idea of moving into tractor design in the 1920s but this plan largely came to nothing and was put on the back burner until the later stages of World War II. After a series of tests in 1946, his first design, the Universal, made its debut some two year later. Farmers were offered two versions—the four-wheeled M4 and the tricycle M3. The original model were petrol driven but the

Universal was later offered with a diesel engine

The Universal 3 was revealed in 1957 and the Universal 4/60 appeared four years later. As Nuffields were beginning to look their age, they underwent a makeover in the mid-1960s, when Nuffield introduced the 10-42 and 10-60 models. These, in turn, were redesigned in 1967 but by then Nuffield was undergoing a major transformation. The company merged with the Austin Motor Company to create the British Leyland Motor Company and Nuffield's tractors were rebranded as Leylands. Leyland developed types like the 270 and 344 Models but was chronically underfunded and was eventually sold in 1981.

One of the more unusual English tractor manufacturers was Roadless Traction Limited, which was found in 1919 by an ex-military man, Lieutenant-Colonel Henry Johnson, who had experience with tanks in World War I and steam engines. In the 1920s Johnson set to work on converting existing lorries into half-tracks and business boomed. The company now turned its attentions to the conversion of tractors. It linked up with a conventional manufacturer, Peter Brotherhood Limited and modified its Peterbro design. Few ever saw the light of day but Roadless persevered and struck up a relationship with another firm, Barford and Perkins Limited, producing a half-tracked variant of the latter's THD design.

The turning point came with the development of rubber-jointed track and Roadless came up with the E track system that could be easily fitted to a wide range of conventional tractors, most notably the Rushton built by AEC. The Roadless Rushton design was popular but Rushton went out of business but Fordson was on hand to help out. Roadless began to convert the Fordson Model N from 1931 and the association between the two would last into the 1980s in one form or another. In the immediate aftermath of World War II Roadless conversions focused on the Fordson E27N and stayed in production until 1964. Other conversions of note were Fordson's Model E and Diesel Major. Roadless had similar relationships with two other U.S. companies, including Case and International Harvester

Roadless began to falter in the late 1970s, largely because of the arrival of similar but cheaper products from companies in Europe, such as Same of Italy, Belarus Tractors of Belarus and Zetor of the Czech Republic, as well as similar product from major U.S. manufacturers, like Caterpillar. Roadless tried to diversify but was hard hit by the recession of the early 1980s and went into voluntary liquidation.

German tractor manufacturing followed a similar pattern, with early pioneer either going to the wall or being bought out. Deutz, for example, was involved in the development of the internal combustion engine and went on to release a string of tractors including the ground-breaking diesel-engined MTZ 222 of 1926. It set out to acquire other companies, such as Fahr and, but it eventually suffered the same fate, being bought first by another German company in 1985 and then by the U.S. company AGCO in 1990. Lanz, the other leading German tractor manufacturer before World War II, introduced such popular designs as the various Bulldog models that were exported to Britain, but it was acquired by John Deere. Fendt, another key manufacturer with a considerable pedigree, survived a little longer and was bought out by AGCO in 1997.

Yet some European manufacturers due survive—for a while. Benz first built tractors in 1919 and produced their first diesel-engined design, the Benz-Sendling in 1923. Three years later Benz merged with Daimler and took the name Mercedes-Benz.

It continued to produce tractors but on a relatively small scale and production only really took off after the end of World War II. It went on to produce such designs as the MAN 325 and the MD-trac. Mercedes-Benz eventually decided to end tractor manufacture, however.

Tractor manufacturers can be found elsewhere in Europe. Fiat, the Italian motor company, began producing tractors immediately after World War I and the Model 702 of 1919 became the first mass-produced design. Fiat went on to produce further designs, such as the Model 708C and Model 40 but its output was rocked by World War II and it did not regain full production until 1950 with the Fiat 55. Fiat tractor division began to expand rapidly thereafter and in 1974 it entered into a joint venture with U.S. company Allis-Chalmers to form Fiat-Allis.

Fiat now embarked on a round of acquisitions to gain a greater foothold in the lucrative North American market, taking over Hesston of Kansas in 1977 and then Agrifull. In 1988 there was a further round of reorganization and Fiat-Allis was merged into FiatGeotech. This next took over Ford New Holland Incorporated in 1991, a move that ended Ford's links with tractor building and FiatGeotech became New Holland Incorporated two years later. Fiat had thus made itself a world player in tractor manufacture in North America but it was not to last long and New Holland was bought out by CNH Global in 1999.

The other Italian tractor builder of note is Landini, a company that can claim to be the country's most long-standing manufacturer. It was founded by Giovanni Landini but it was his sons would create the first Italian tractor in 1925. Other followed, including models known as Buffalo, Velite and Super. After World War II, Landini began to introduce new designs, such as the L25 and 55L of the 1950s. Landini continued to produce tractors under its own name but was actually taken over by Massey-Ferguson in 1960 but in 1989 the latter sold two-thirds of its holding. Yet the company had continued to expand both at home and overseas and it has even made some inroads into the tough U.S. market, where is designs are distributed through AGCO.

French tractor production is dominated by Renault, which started out building crawlers after gaining experience in tank construction during World War I. The turning point came in 1933 when the VY tractor emerged and went on to be the first successful diesel tractor to be sold in France. Renault built tractors to support the country's war effort during World War II and continued to manufacture new designs into the present day. These included such units as the Model 61 RS, and the Model 106.

Eastern Europe has also seen its fair share of tractor manufacturers but perhaps the most successful is little-known Zetor, which was found in what is now known as the Czech Republic in 1946. It has been a remarkably successful company, selling something like 500,000 tractors to more than 100 countries. This effort was partly due to a series of marketing alliances with companies like the Motokov Group and John Deere. It has also granting manufacturing licenses to other foreign companies so Zetor machines can be found in many guises.

PIONEERS OF THE SUPERTRACTOR

Supertractors, those monsters of the farmyard, are not about speed but about power and the ability to get the job done as quickly as possible. The statistics speak for themselves—an average 100hp modern tractor can plough around two acres an hour but a 500hp supertractor can do the same in just two minutes. Yet such big tractors can only really be used profitably on the biggest farms, where their higher purchase price and running costs are offset by the higher work rate that a very large acreage demands.

It is perhaps not surprising then that much, if not all, of the impetus behind the development of the first supertractors came from the plains of the U.S. Midwest and Canada. Many of those first manufacturing companies began as small, often homegrown enterprises. Wagner, Steiger, Versatile and Big Bud were the early pioneers of supertractors between the 1950s and 1960s but many of these companies had somewhat checkered careers, and suffered badly during times of economic recession when farmers cut back on their capital spending. Some of the pioneers

went under but others survived in one form or another—but usually as part of a bigger manufacturing business.

What is a supertractor? Ideally, a design has to have several key elements to qualify for the title. First, it has to have an articulated chassis with pivot-steering; second, a powerful diesel engine throwing an awful lot of horsepower; third, it must be four-wheel drive with same-sized wheels. None of these elements is especially new, however. Pivot-steering was actually developed in the 1920s with Lanz, for example, introducing a pivot-steering variant of its Bulldog design. Four-wheel drive dates back even farther with the U.S. firm Olmstead of Montana marketing the Four-Wheel Pull tractor in 1912. Thus all of the

key components needed were developed in earlier times but they were not brought together in one machine until after World War II.

The momentum towards building the first true supertractor grew as engine horsepower began to rise. The best tractor of the 1930s had 40hp, but this output rose successively after 1945. John Deere, for example, released the 51hp Model R in 1949, Oliver's 70hp Super 99 followed in 1955 and Allis-Chalmers produced the first 100hp tractor, the D21, in 1963. Yet this increase in power had a downside—as the power output increased it was difficult to transmit all of it to the ground through two-wheel drive, even if the tractor had multi-speed transmissions.

Tractors inevitably began to suffer wheel slip, especially in wet and muddy conditions, and this of course impacted on farming efficiency as it wasted time and fuel.

Manufacturers came up with a number of solutions to the problem. One rather costly idea was the tandem-tractor concept in which a pair of tractors was brought together with the driver sitting in the rear one, which had had its front wheels removed. Various companies build conversion packs but English dealer Ernest Doe actually linked two Fordson Majors together to create the Doe Triple-D. Such tractors never really caught on, although the Triple D was available until 1966, largely because there were considerably simpler and more elegant solutions to the problem of traction.

It was possible to fit double or even triple rear wheels to a standard tractor and this became the common response to the traction issue in the late 1960s and early 1970s. However, there were other technical advances that were coming to grips with the issue from another direction. There was an early form of four-wheel drive known as front-wheel assist, essentially a powered front axle with small wheels. This, of course helped with traction but what was really needed was four equally sized wheels. Increasing the number of rear wheels and fitting front-wheel assist could only take the story so far but increases in horsepower were ongoing and a more permanent solution was really needed.

The idea of four-wheel drive pivot-steering was developed by Elmer Wagner in 1949. Elmer was one of seven brothers who had founded Wagner Tractors Inc. in Portland, Oregon. The first such tractor, Wagner's TR-6, did not make an appearance until 1955 but this 64-horsepower machine was superseded by the 85hp TR-9 and this was in turn replaced by the 160hp TR-14. Wagner great leap forward was to apply articulation or pivot-steering to a tractor and this made his designs much more maneuverable that those of his rivals. Basically, a tractor with articulation is split down the middle, has two fixed axles and pivots on two hydraulic rams that give it a turning angle of some 40 degrees to the left and right. Pivot-steering also allows for both axles to move up and down independently up to 15 degrees and

obviously permits the use of four large wheels. All of this means that more power is transmitted to bigger tires that, within the aforementioned limits, will be in contact with the ground all of the time.

Wagner was soon a profitable business and was bought by the FWD Corporation in 1961. A new range of supertractors, the Wagner WA (Wagner Agricultural) series was introduced. The WA-6, WA-9, WA-14 and WA-24 were not greatly different from their forebears but were later given more powerful engines. FWD Corporation decided to get out of tractor production and Wagner passed, albeit briefly, into the hands of Raygo, who produced the WA-24. John Deere now stepped in, signing a contract with Wagner in early 1968 to build 100 W-14s and WA-17s in Deere's own livery. Wagner delivered just 51 supertractors but sales were poor and Deere dropped the contract in 1970. A clause in the contract forbade Wagner from selling a rival farm tractor for five years and the company was forced to close.

However, Wagner's pioneering days led to further entries into the supertractor field as the big farmers of North America soon cottoned on to the value of their designs. Douglas and Morris Steiger, dairy farmers from Minnesota, came up with their own supertractor design for their personal use during the winter of 1958–1959. The Steiger No. 1, which was nicknamed "Barney" as it was literally built like a barn, was made up from various bit and pieces, including a 238-horsepower Detroit Diesel engine, and became so popular that neighbouring farmers asked for something similar. The Steigesr subsequently went into fulltime if limited production in 1961. Things really took off two years later when three Detroit Deisel-engined machines, the 1250, 1700 and 2200, rolled off the production line.

Their small farm was not really geared up for mass production and in 1969 the brothers, who were now backed by a financial consortium, moved to a redundant tank factory in Fargo, North Dakota. Their first Series I supertractors emerged and were given the names of big cats, such as Wildcat, Super Wildcat, Tiger, Bearcat and Cougar. Something like one third of North American farmers buying supertractors were soon opting for Steigers. Series II followed from 1974, when the older tractor

INTRODUCTION

were upgrade except for the Wildcat, which was deemed too small and was replaced by a new design, the Panther.

Steiger also began selling their design to other tractor manufacturers who simply rebadged them and gave them a new livery. Canadian Co-op Implements, for example, bought Steigers in the early 1970s did away with their lime-green paint scheme and repainted them in their company's orange. Equally, the Allis-Chalmers 440 of 1972–1975 was a Steiger design as was Ford's extensive FW series (1977–1985), if in slightly modified form. Steiger continued to create new design under its own badge, however. Series III came in 1976—and by the end of the decade the company had built some 10,000 supertractors—while Series IV along with the new 1000 range arrived in 1983.

Yet dales soon dropped alarmingly as recession forced farmers to cut back on expenditure and in 1986 Steiger was made bankrupt. The firm was bought by the owners of Case-IH, Tenneco, who soon dropped the distinctive lime-green livery for their own red and black, and replaced the big cat names with blander numerical designations. The Bearcat, for example, became the 9130 but Tenneco finally relented in 1995 and the Steiger badge, if not the paint scheme, returned.

Wagner and Steiger were the pioneers of the supertractor concept but they were soon far from alone as in 1966 a Canadian company, Versatile, came up with their 125hp D100. Versatile, a well-established company founded by Peter Pakosh in 1946, took a lead over both Wagner and Steiger as the D100 had most of the attributed of a supertractor but cost the same as a more conventional design. The D100 proved extremely popular and Versatile successively produced a number of more powerful models designated the D118, G125 and D145, and were collectively known as Series I Versatiles. Series II emerged between 1974 and 1976 and included the 700, 800, 850 and 900 models. The latter was a leap forward for the company as it was comparable in size to those being produced by Steiger.

Series II was subsequently expanded to include four more supertractors, including the Model 950, which remained in production until 1982, but even this was dwarfed by the 600hp "Big Roy" prototype that was built in the latter part of the decade. Versatile was sold to Cornat Industries in 1977 and the company produced the new Labour Force range the next year to replace the Series II types which ultimately consisted of the Models 835, 855, 875, 895 (from 1980) and 935. Series III, later known as the Designation 6 Series, began to emerge in 1983 and included Models 756, 945, 955, 975 and 1150.

Yet Versatile was by now in trouble, a victim of agricultural recession. John Deere was a potential buyer but Ford New Holland's bid was accepted in 1987. Versatile supertractors continued to appear in the original yellow and red livery but soon received Ford blue, although a small Versatile badge was kept. Ford sold New Holland along with Versatile to Fiat. The Versatile 80 Series (Models 9280, 9480, 9680, and 9880) was introduced in 1994 and then replaced by the more powerful 82 Series. New Holland merged with Case to form CNH Global in 2000 but was then hived off to Buhler Industries based in Winnipeg. The latter relaunched Versatile supertractors in their original livery during early 2001 but this was soon dropped in favor of the company's own red and black. Buhler began producing a new five-supertractor 2000 Series in 2006.

Another of the first supertractor pioneers was Willie Hensler, who ran a Wagner dealership in Havre, Montana. He was left without anything to sell when Wagner collapsed so Hensler and his business partner, Bud Nelson, set up their own Northern Manufacturing Company in the summer of 1968. Nelson was the designer and the supertractors were known as "Big Bud" and the first series was designated HN for Hensler-Nixon. These were not especially revolutionary designs but they were certainly bigger than their rivals. The HN-250 arrived in 1969 but farmers were looking for ever more powerful supertractors and the HN-250 arrived the following year and the HN-350 in 1973. Big Bud next introduced the KT-450 design in 1976 and this was followed by the KT-400 and KT-525.

The company experimented with the Big Bud 16V-747 but only one was ever built. Others designs were more commercially successful, including the Series 3 in 1979. This is believed to have been the company's most lucrative series of all and consisted of some 16 different configurations. Yet the series was something of a swansong as smaller companies like Big Bud struggled to compete with larger manufacturers, particularly in times of recession. The company filed for bankruptcy in 1982. Meissner Tractors, also of Havre, bought Big Bud and began producing Series 4 supertractors in 1985 but output was slow and sales sluggish. The plant was closed in 1991, an event marking the demise of yet another supertractor pioneer.

MASS PRODUCING THE SUPERTRACTOR

The pioneers of supertractors had mostly been small-scale producers and for a few years they had a virtually monopoly in the market for such machines but all that began to change as long-established and bigger manufacturers saw supertractors as another market to exploit. The new entrants into the field often had one overwhelming advantage—economies of scale, which was often brought about by merging with or buying small- and medium-sized firms. They were thus able to built supertractors like the pioneers but their unit costs were considerably less, not least because they could use off-the-shelf components and had a well-established network of dealerships to sell them through. The large manufacturers were also better equipped to ride out the recessions that periodically bedevilled farming.

One of the first medium-sized manufacturers to take up the challenge of supertractor design was International Harvester, who produced their first model, the International 4300, in 1960. This was the most powerful supertractor of the day with 300hp but it sales were somewhat sluggish. The next model, the International 4100 of 1965, enjoyed better sales but its replacement, 1969's International 4156, proved considerably less popular. International Harvester took a sizeable stake in Steiger in the early 1970s and this led to the 4366 in 1973 and this sold a very commendable 3000-plus units. The 4366 was a more powerful upgrade but sold comparatively poorly.

International Harvester also produced its 86 Pro-Ag range in the mid-1970s, which consisted of updates of its existing models renamed 4386 and 4586, and a wholly new model, the 4786. The company what badly hit by recession and was forced to sell its holdings in Steiger to the Deutz Corporation but it did manage to produce another design in 1979, the 2+2 358. This proved to be a massive hit and International Harvester sold something like 3000 in just two years. The original 50 Series of 2+2s was upgraded in 1982 with the arrival of the 60 Series, which comprised the 6388, 6588 and 6788 models, but sales were slow. Some Super 70 Series models were produced but production as halted soon after International Harveseter was bought by Case in 1985.

Although a large number of North American tractor manufacturers went under or merged during the 1960s, one managed to retain a measure of independence until the latter part of the decade—Minneapolis-Moline and Oliver. The latter had actually been bought by the truck-building White Motor Corporation in 1960 and Minneapolis-Moline was purchased just three year later. Minneapolis-Moline and Oliver produced two main supertractors, the A4T-1400 and A4T-1600 in 1969, that were sold under a number of guises. They were offered in Oliver's green livery as the Oliver 2455 and 2655, for example.

White, which was renamed White Farm Equipment, in 1969 launched its own Field Boss Range in 1974 but offered them in only its own silver and charcoal grey livery, a decision effectively marking the demise of Minneapolis-Moline and Oliver. The company upgraded the 4-150 Field Boss in 1979 to produce the 4-175 and this was soon followed by the 4-180.White Farming Equipment, however, in financial difficulty by the end of the decade and its tractor manufacturing arm was purchased by the TIC Investment Corporation. Production resumed but the White name and livery were abandoned in 1982 and replaced by the WFE logo and a white with red stripe livery. TIC sold WFE to Allied Products in 1985 and a new company—White-New Idea—emerged. The White supertractors brand was soon dropped and White-New Idea was itself bought by the AGCO in 1993

Allis-Chalmers took its time to produce a supertractor and did not stay in the market for very long. The company initially bought in the Steiger Bearcat beginning in 1972, gave it an orange paint job and rebranded it as the A-C 440. The first home-grown model, the A-C 7580, was announced in 1975 but it was hardly revolutionary and to a large extent used pre-existing components from Allis-Chalmers' two-wheel drive 7000 Series. The A-C 7580 only really just scraped into the supertractor class and the company soon found there was a demand for more powerful types. This resulted in 1978's much bigger and more powerful A-C 8550.

The company introduced a major new series, the 4W-220 and 4W-305, in 1982 to replace the 7580 and 8550, yet it was soon beset by problems. Some of its more conventional models could do the work of its smaller supertractors and, of course, cost less to buy. Allis-Chalmers sought to cut costs and the 4W-220 was dropped in 1984 but this made little difference. The company sold its agricultural arm to Deutz the next year. The surviving 4W-305 was rebranded as a Deutz-Allis machine but sales were hardly earth-shattering and production was subsequently abandoned.

John Deere tested the supertractor market with the 8010 and 8020 models that were produced between 1959 and 1965 but they proved hard to sell and the former was plagued with mechanical problems. Despite this early setback and a short-lived associated with Steiger, the company returned to producing its own supertractors and came up with the 20 Series 7020 in 1970 and the more powerful 7520 the next year Both designs were relatively cheap to manufacture and offered easy handling. Yet farmers were demanding ever more power and a better sound proofed cab and both of these issues were addressed with the 30 Series 8430 and 8630 models that made their debut in the mid-1970s.

Deere now embarked on a regular pattern of new supertractor introductions—the 40 Series, which were only a slight improvement on the 30 Series, followed in 1979, the 50 Series, which used an in-house 370hp engine, followed in 1982 and the 60 Series, which returned to a bought-in Cummins engine, arrived in 1988. Although Deere had introduced three new series of supertractors in the space of a decade or so, it had also faced serious economic problems and had gone through a period of redundancies and cutbacks that might have pushed a smaller firm under.

It did survive and went on to produce the four-model 70 Series from 1993 and the 90 Series three year later. The 70 Series was very much an interim design but the 90 Series was a wholly new product that made use of Deere's own PowerTech range of six-cylinder diesel engines. Deere also responded to Caterpillar's Challenger, a rubber-tracked supertractor, and offered a similar option with its 9300T and 9400T models. The 90 Series was a considerable success and a five-model update, the 9020, was introduced in the early 2000s.

Massey Ferguson was no pioneer in the race to develop supertractors and came to the party rather late. It was not until 1971 that the company produced its first models, the MF 1500 and MF 1800. These were followed by the MF 1200, a design produced by the company's British arm and released in 1972. It was something of a original, being the first four-wheeled drive machine to be seen in numbers by British farmers. These original two designs from 1971 were somewhat underpowered by existing supertractor standards and the first updates of the two designs, 1975's MF 1505 and MF 1805, were given larger engines. The MF 1200 also under went a belated upgrade in 1979, the MF 1250, but, although the range sold well overall, it was discontinued in 1982.

Massey Ferguson had so far concentrated production in the light to medium ranges of supertractors and lacked a real heavyweight. This all changed to a degree with their MF 4000 Series that was released between 1978 and 1980. There were four models in the series and they were all powered by a Cummins engine. The 4000 Series remained in production until 1986 whereupon Massey Ferguson introduced a major upgrade with the 5200 Series. In truth, however, this series was the company's last hurrah with supertractors and they were built by a specialist manufacturer, McConnell. The exclusive deal lasted less than three years and in 1991 McConnell began selling them in their own yellow livery rather than the red of Massey Ferguson. The latter company was taken over by AGCO in 1994 and concentrated on smaller tractors.

CNH Global is a huge concern, one that grew out of various acquisitions and mergers involving the likes of Case, International

Harvester and New Holland among others. The company emerged in its present form in 1999 when Case merged with New Hampshire. Case in particular had a supertractor pedigree stretching back to 1964's 1200 Traction King. A new model, the 1470 Traction King, appeared in 1969, the year that Tenneco took over the company, and the 2470 Traction King made it debut two year later. Case continued to build ever more powerful designs, including the 2670 Tractor King of 1974. The 70 Series was by know a little long in the tooth and Case developed the three-model 90 Series as a replacement, although the 4490, 4690 and 4890 were little more than updates in reality. A further update followed in 1985 with the 94 Series. This again comprised three models, the 4494, 4696 and 4894.

Tenneco had been making several acquisitions during this period—International Harvester in 1985 and the venerable Steiger two years later. Operating under the name of Case-IH focussed on producing rebadged and renamed Steiger designs—the Puma became the Case IH-9110 and the Lion became the Case IH-9180, for example. An update 9200 Series made its debut in 1990 and the 9300 Series in 1995, which also saw the return of the Steiger badge. Two year later Case-IH made a foray into track-driven machines with the Quadtrac, a supertractor inspired by Caterpillar's Challenger rubber-tracked machine.

Case IH next went on to merge with New Holland, itself a producer of supertractors. These were initially based on the Ford Versatile types but in 1994 these were replaced by the 80 Series. These were badged as New Holland machines from 1997 and upgraded to produce the follow-on 82 Series. These were supplanted by the 84 Series two year later, when New Holland was bought by Case-IH to form CNH Global. For a while the company produced models by both Case-IH and New Holland but rationalization was soon needed. The outcome was the Case-IH STX of 2000 which was also sold in a slightly modified form as the TJ Series in the New Holland livery of blue and black rather than Case-IH's red and black from the next year.

AGCOSTAR was also one of the major players in supertractors, even though it was a very later entrant into the field. Its story really began in 1990, when Deutz-Allis was purchased from its German parent company by its U.S. management led by Robert Ratcliff Gleaner was also bought the same year and AGCO was born. It then embarked on a rapid expansion plan during the early 1990s that left it with its own manufacturing plant. The turning point came in 1994 when it bought Massey Ferguson and thereby became an international brand. The same year AGCO moved into the business of building supertractors by snapping up the McConnell Manufacturing Company.

The decision was taken to create a new supertractor brand and the company came up with the AGCOSTAR badge and launched its first model, the 8425, in 1995. A smaller model, the 8360, made its debut the next year but thereafter development stalled. However, Caterpillar came to AGCO's rescue in 2002 and the latter bought the rights to manufacture the former's rubber-tracked Challenger but this signaled the end for the earlier AGCOSTARs. The family-owned British company JCB developed its own type of supertractor in the late 1970s and the first Fastrac design made its public debut in 1991. As the name suggests JCB aimed to produce a supertractor appropriate for European conditions, one that could reach high speeds on roads rather than have pure pulling power. The Fastrac originally came in two versions, the 120 and 145, but these were soon upgraded to give the 125, 135 and 150 models. The yet more powerful 185 design followed but JCB then turned to a wholly new series of supertractors that were better at field work. These were 1995's 1100 Series, consisting of the 1115 and 1135 models. The 1100 Series had a larger turning circle than more conventional types and JCB opted to work on the problem and developed the Quadtronic four-wheel system for steering the vehicle. A new, more sophisticated range, the 2000/3000 Series came into production in 1998 and the company introduced a more radical design in 2005, the Fastrac 8250, that still kept the speed of the earlier designs but also had a much-improved horsepower.

AGCO

AGCO was born when the US management of the Deutz-Allis corporation bought out the North American side of the company and renamed it AGCO (Allis-Gleaner Company). Tractors are distributed under the AGCO Allis name. AGCO acquired White in 1991, Massey Ferguson in 1994, Fendt in 1997, Caterpillar's Challenger line in 2002, and Valtra (formerly Valmet) in 2002. In 2001, The AGCO White and AGCO Allis names were dropped in favour of the AGCO brand.

The AGGO product line brings together some of the longest-running and most trusted names in the business, including GLEANER, Hesston, Sunflower and White Planters. Looking for state-of-the-art solutions? They're all here, including AGCO high-horsepower tractors with PowerMaxx CVT™, Hesston big square balers and the new GLEANER A85 Class VIII combine.

AGCO views its new tractors as an opportunity to push the company's brand name forward and combine two tractor lines into one. The company uses its Allis Chalmers heritage for the tractor's color scheme. To balance the family tree, the tractors draw on the White heritage by being outfitted with Cummins diesel engines and a silver emphasis in the tractor decal. The machines are available in three series, spanning 70 PTO hp to 225 PTO hp. The model number corresponds with the PTO horsepower of the tractor.

AGCO

RT SERIES

ARMATRAK

Erkunt Agricultural Machinery Industries Inc. started the production of agricultural tractors in September 2004; as a subsidiary of Erkunt Industries Inc., one of the biggest casting and machinery production companies in Europe; known for its high technology standards and experience that goes beyond half a century.

The company has extended its production line from 2 to 15 different models in a very short time in response to a very quickly increasing level of demand. Those tractors truly live up to the top-of-the-line reputation they have established with their high technology, economic and environment- friendly EURO 2 engines, 16 forward – 8 reverse gear transmissions (ZF T537, produced by Erkunt Agricultural Machinery Industries Inc. under the "ZF" license), high performance deliverance even in low horsepower levels, a top speed of 40 km/h (30 miles per hour), 30-40% less fuel consumption in comparison with the competition and 6 attractive color alternatives.

Erkunt Agricultural Machinery Ind. Inc. presents its products on the international market under the ArmaTrac brand. In order to meet the different needs of farmers, ArmaTrac offers 60HP, 70 HP and 80 HP tractors with 2 or 4 wheel drive options; providing a choice of cabin or shade in addition.

BUHLER

Versatile had its roots with the Hydraulic Engineering Company of Toronto, which was founded in 1947 making small agricultural implements. The company expanded, and opened a factory in Winnipeg, which was later to be used for tractors. In 1963, the Hydraulic Engineering Company offered shares to the public and renamed to Versatile.

Versatile's focus was large four-wheel drive tractors, much like Steiger.

In addition to high horsepower tractors, the company had great success with the 150 "Push-Pull". This tractor could be operated in either direction, and featured an operator's seat the rotated 180 degrees.

The depressed farm market forced Versatile to stop operations in 1986. The company was purchased by Ford-New Holland and resumed operations in 1988, although with New Holland colors. With the merger of CaseIH and New Holland

in 1999, the Winnipeg factory was closed and the Versatile name dropped. In 2001, Buhler Indutries acquired the Winnipeg factory and the rights to the Versatile name. The corporation currently builds four-wheel drive tractors under the Buhler Versatile brand, in the traditional red and yellow Versatile paint.

CASE

Case IH Tractors are currently manufactured by CNH Global, CNH is the abbreviation for Case-New Holland and the majority owner of the CNH Global is the Fiat automotive conglomerate. Currently, CNH operates under the names Case IH, Case Construction, Kobelco and New Holland which each operate as different operating divisions. Case IH markets tractors and agricultural equipment. Case Construction markets construction equipment from skid steers to large front loaders. Kobelco markets construction equipment, particularly known for manufacturing excavators. New Holland markets both agricultural and construction equipment.

Case IH currently markets compact utility tractors, for landscape and property maintenance, under the brand name Case IH - DX Series Farmall. The Case IH - DX Series Farmall compact utility tractors are nearly clones of the New Holland Boomer series tractors. Case IH also markets larger tractors aimed at the agricultural market under the brand names Case IH and Steiger. Despite the fact that the compact utility tractors marketed by Case IH are nearly identical to the New Holland Boomer series tractors, many of the larger agricultural tractors marketed by these two respective brand names are unique to those brands.

The Case IH name originates from Case Corporation and International Harvester, both predecessors to CNH Global. In 1985 Tenneco purchased most of the agricultural equipment assets from the International Harvester Company and merged them with their company, J.I. Case to form the Case IH brand. In 1999 Case Corporation merged with New Holland to form CNH Global N.V. The brand Case IH is now used for agricultural equipment, whereas the brand Case or Case CE is used for construction equipment.

CLAAS

CLAAS is an agricultural machinery manufacturer based in Harsewinkel/ Germany in the region of North Rhine Westphalia. CLAAS agricultural products are usually sold under the CLAAS name, except in North America where CLAAS combines are distributed as LEXIONcombines by Caterpillar dealers. The CLAAS product range includes combine harvesters, forage harvesters, balers, mowers, rakes, tedders and other harvesting machines.

In 2004, CLAAS purchased the Renault Agricultural division from the France-based Renault company.

The Claas Axion is the new tractor built by the Claas-owned former Renault tractor plant at Le Mans. The 163 - 225 hp (ECE R24) tractor containing a John Deere engine and the Hexashift transmission with six ranges and four powershift stages. In its earliest stages of production it was known by its codename ET 97. Development work started for the new Axion in 2003.

DEUTZ-FAHR

Deutz can trace its history to the Nikolaus Otto, Gottlieb Daimler, and the first internal combustion engines. Agricultural machinery production began in 1907. Deutz tractors were very popular in western Europe after World War II, farmers liked the simple, rugged air-cooled diesel engines. In 1969, Deutz mergered with Fahr, a farm implement manufacturer and the Deutz-Fahr brand was born. The company was purchased by SAME in 1995.

In 1969, KHD (Klockner-Humboldt-Deutz) purchased the KÖLA company, a German-based manufacturer of combines. Other joint ventures or cooperations included the Agrale-Deutz, with the Agrale tractor company; collaborations with the Indian Kirloskar company, manufacturer of engines and tractors; MeMo, a German company that exported Deutz-based tractors to the USA; PMA in Algeria;

owned 30% of the Steiger company after International Harvester sold out; Torpedo, which built licensed tractors, sometimes under the Torpedo Deutz name; and tractechnik, (from Deutz Intrac's). In Canada, Deutz-Fahr tractors were sometimes sold under the Co-op Implements name through a co-op of dealers. KHD moved to grow the company with the purchase of the assets of the Allis-Chalmers company in 1985, which included the Gleaner combines. Allis-Chalmers traces its roots to the Monarch, Advance-Rumely and Gleaner companies. The Allis-Chalmers name was retired, and it became Deutz-Allis.

KHD and Deutz-Allis struggled financially, and Deutz-Fahr sold the North American operations to a newly formed group, the Gleaner-Allis Corporation, later changed to Allis Gleaner Corporation, or

AGCO, in 1990. Deutz-Fahr continued having problems, and sold the Argentine operations to AGCO in 1997, including the Argentine engine business.

In 1995, KHD sold Deutz-Fahr to S-L-H, or SAME, which renamed itself Same Deutz-Fahr (SDF). The combine business was discontinued and out-sourced to AGCO. All Deutz-Fahr combines were then built at AGCO's Dronningborg factory in Denmark. SDF purchased the Deutz AG engine business from the former KHD in 2003, and then purchased the uro akovic combine business in Croatia, which built combines licensed from Deutz-Fahr. DF had a joint venture in Argentina and built combines under the Deutz-Araus brand. AGCO later discontinued that brand and sold the Araus name to the Metalfor company.

AGROTRON TTV

FENDT

Fendt is a German manufacturer of agricultural tractors and machines. It is part of AGCO Corporation. It was founded in 1937 by Xaver Fendt and purchased by AGCO in 1997. Fendt manufactures and markets a full line of tractors, and recently began selling combines built by AGCO and Laverda. Fendt also developed the Vario gearbox which is one of the most advanced tractor gearboxes. It is also used in JCB and Massey Ferguson machines.

The vario gearbox was first developed in the 1970s but due to lack of funding it was never seen on a production tractor until 1996 when fendt launced the revolutionary Fendt 926 vario. this was the first ever stepless transmission to be launched onto the tractor market, and still is the only ever true stepless transmission with brands such as John Deere and New Holland trying to make a piece of machinery as advanced as a Fendt. When put into a tractor the gearbox electronics can be "tweaked" to make this tractor go much faster than its electronically limited 50km/h top speed.

Fendt have just launched the fastest, most powerful conventional tractor ever, the Fendt Vario 936. This has all of the technology featured in the previous tractors plus a little bit more. These tractors are capable of speeds of 65km/h and are rated at 360hp(DIN)

Fendt are widely regarded as being the 'Rolls-Royce' of tractors, in terms of build quality, technology and customer service, however they are generally priced higher than the competition although some higher spec European John Deere / Massey Ferguson machines may be of similar quality.

FENDT

HÜRLIMANN

The Swiss manufacturer Hurlimann was an early pioneer of direct-injection diesel. In 1975, Hurlimann was acquired by SAME. The brand continues today, although the tractors are nearly identical to their SAME and Lamborghini counterparts.

Erkunt Agricultural Machinery Industries Inc. started the production of agricultural tractors in September 2004; as a subsidiary of Erkunt Industries Inc., one of the biggest casting and machinery production companies in Europe; known for its high technology standards and experience that goes beyond half a century.

JOHN DEERE

Deere & Company was founded in 1868 by blacksmith John Deere. Deere had achieved great success in 1837 when he built a plow from highly polished steel. Deere & Company entered the tractor manufacturing business in 1918. Deere sold a small number of tractors designed by Joseph Dain, with limited success. That same year, Deere purchased the Waterloo Gasoline Traction Engine Company, that built the Waterloo Boy tractor. In late 1923, John Deere introduced the Model D, which remained in production for the next 30 years. Deere became a dominant force in tractor production with the 4020 in 1963.

There are six different types of agricultural John Deere Tractors:

- Compact Utility Tractors, which are mainly used for lawn care and maintenance.
- Row-Crop Tractors, which are mainly used for work on agricultural farms.
- Speciality Tractors, which are mainly used for work on small farms, also known as a hobby farm.
- Utility Tractors, which are mainly used for smaller activities on an agricultural farm such as hay bailing, raking or moving implements.
- Four-Wheel Drive Tractors, which are mainly used for pulling implements that require extra power such as a large plow or disk bine.
- Track Series, which are also mainly used on agricultural farms for pulling implements that require extra power.

LAMBORGHINI

Ferruccio Lamborghini started building tractors in Italy in the late 1940s. Initially, the tractors were built using a mixture of surplus military hardware from World War Two. By 1954, Lamborghini was building its own engines. Also, the company had expanded manufacturing into other areas, notably, high performance sports cars. In the late 1960s Ferrucio became disinterested in tractors, and the firm was formally acquired by SAME in 1971. The Lamborghini name is still used on tractors today, as part of the SAME Deutz-Fahr Group.

MASSEY FERGUSON

The firm was founded in 1847 in Newcastle, Ontario by Daniel Massey as the Newcastle Foundry and Machine Manufactory. The company began making some of the world's first mechanical threshers, first by assembling parts from the United States and eventually designing and building their own equipment. The firm was taken over and expanded by his son Harry Massey who renamed it the Massey Manufacturing Co. and in 1879 moved the company to Toronto where it soon became one of the city's leading employers. The massive collections of factories on King St. W. became one of the best known features of the city. Massey expanded the company and began to sell its products internationally. Through extensive advertising campaigns he made it one of the most well known brands in Canada. The firm owed much of its success to Canadian tariffs that prevented the larger American firms from competing in Canada. A labour shortage throughout the country also made the firm's mechanized equipment very attractive.

Massey Ferguson (under control by AGCO Corporation) have developed a huge range of agricultural vehicles and have a large share in the market across the world especially in Europe. The first real wholesale tractor was the Massey Ferguson TVO which was quickly replaced by the Diesel 20. Proceeding the Diesel 20 came the Massey Ferguson 35 and later 35X. These tractors were massively available and sold across the UK and Ireland in particular.

SAME

Societa Anonima Motori Endotermici (SAME) was founded in the 1920s by Francesco Cassani. Cassani was an early tractor pioneer in Italy, being one of the first to use diesel engines and four-wheel drive in farm equipment. SAME has continuted to grow and expand, acquiring Lamborghini tractors in 1972, Hurlimann in 1977, and Deutz-Fahr in 1995.

The SAME DEUTZ-FAHR Group under the chairmanship of Vittorio Carozza and management of the Chief Executive Officer Massimo Bordi, was founded in 1927 by Francesco Cassani in Treviglio, in the province of Bergamo in northern Italy. With the brands SAME, LAMBORGHINI, DEUTZ-FAHR and HÜRLIMANN, the company is one of the world's leading manufacturers of tractors, combine harvesters, engines and other farm machines.